On each page of this word book is a lively, colourful scene. Lots of things are happening in each picture, to draw the child's attention and stimulate his or her interest and imagination. Some scenes will be familiar ones; some will be more unusual. All have been chosen to intrigue and interest, and to prompt thoughts and questions.

Picked out around the busy scenes are single items, all labelled so that the child can look, point out, identify and say the words out loud. Later, he or she will be able to read the words. The 300 words have been carefully chosen to provide a mixture of familiar and new words—and there is a useful alphabetical word list at the back of the book.

Published by

CHARTWELL BOOKS, INC.
A Division of **BOOK SALES, INC.**
110 Enterprise Avenue
Secaucus, New Jersey 07094
Printed in Italy
SBN 0-89009-732-1

my first book of words

words by Brenda Apsley

pictures by Peter Broadbent

**CHARTWELL
BOOKS, INC.**

house

washbasin

bath

toilet

bathroom

bedroom

kitchen

living room

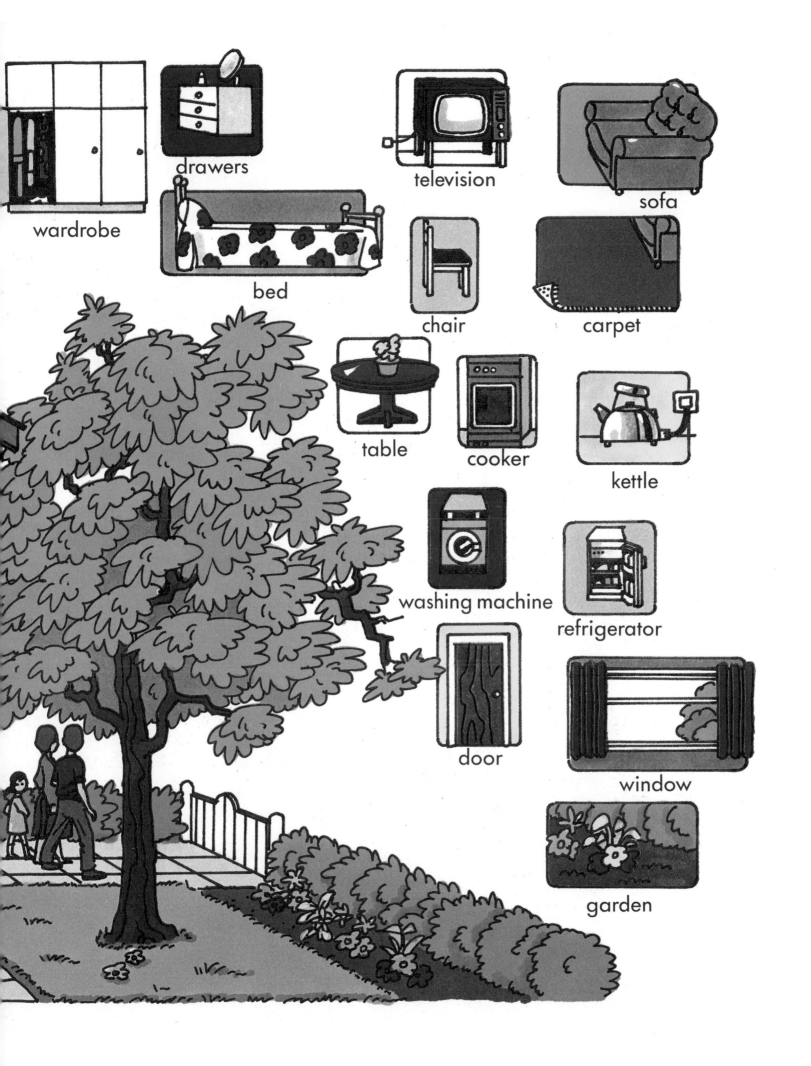

wardrobe

drawers

television

sofa

bed

chair

carpet

table

cooker

kettle

washing machine

refrigerator

door

window

garden

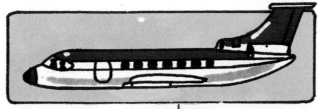
aeroplane

pilot

luggage

air hostess

windsock

control tower

trolley

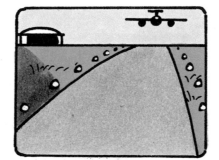
runway

landing lights

helicopter

check-in desk

hangar

fuel truck

airport

farm

barn

sheep

pond

farmer

tractor

hays

field

lambs

calf

geese

pig

horse

hens

plough

goat

donkey

cow

farmhouse

orchard

sheep dog

swing

racing car

robot

dolls' house

puppet

marbles

doll

rocking horse

train

building bricks

soldiers

ball

castle

boat

typewriter

teddy

toy shop

globe

ink

blackboard

ruler

drawing pins

chalk

books

map

paints

brushes

pencils

paper

calendar

desk

teacher

pen

scissors

school

city

bus stop   road sign   car   police car   factory

traffic lights   shop   cinema   crossin

truck

house

church

office block

policeman

taxi

flats

tug

hovercraft

buoy

net

lighthou[se]

crane

warehouse

barge

oil tanker

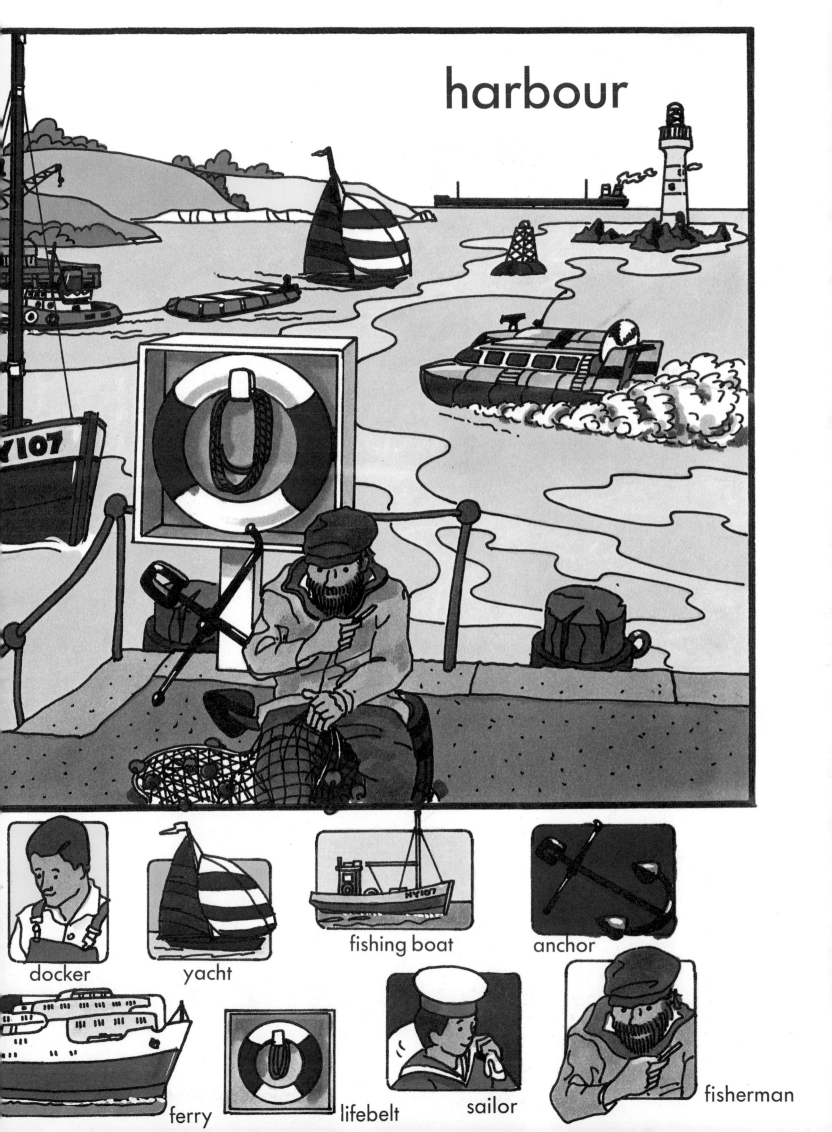

harbour

docker

yacht

fishing boat

anchor

ferry

lifebelt

sailor

fisherman

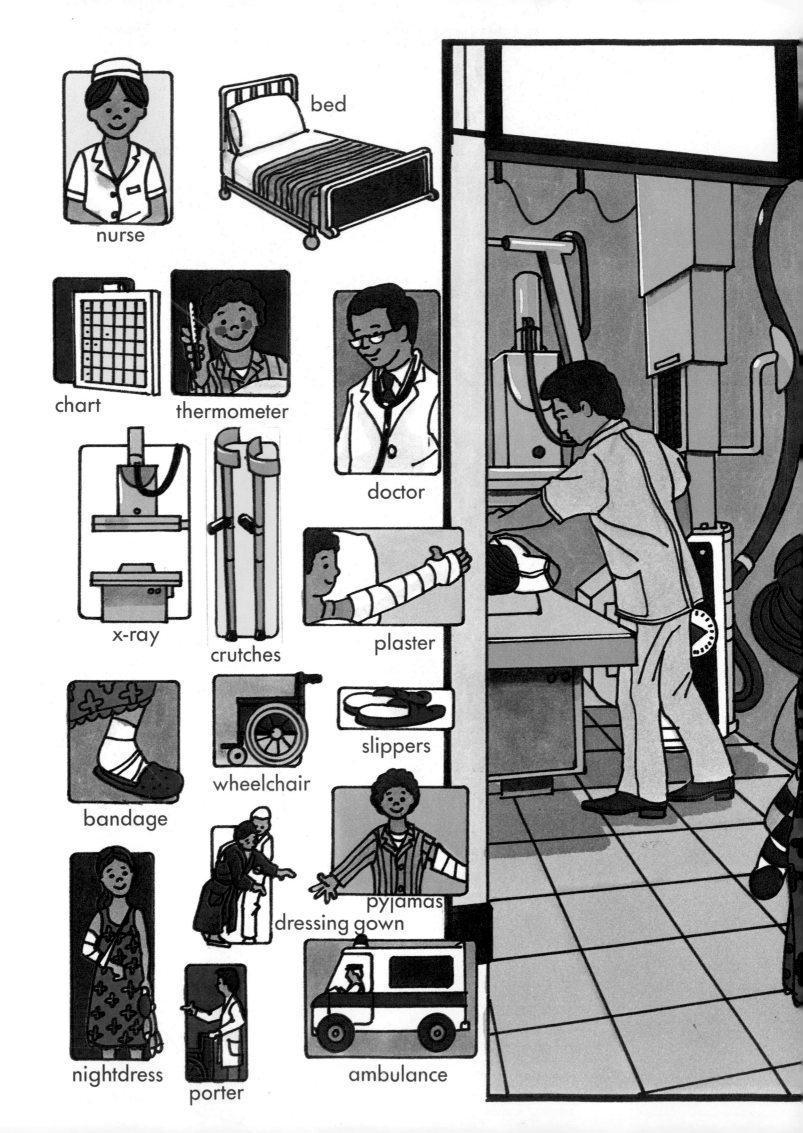

nurse

bed

chart

thermometer

doctor

x-ray

crutches

plaster

bandage

wheelchair

slippers

nightdress

porter

dressing gown

pyjamas

ambulance

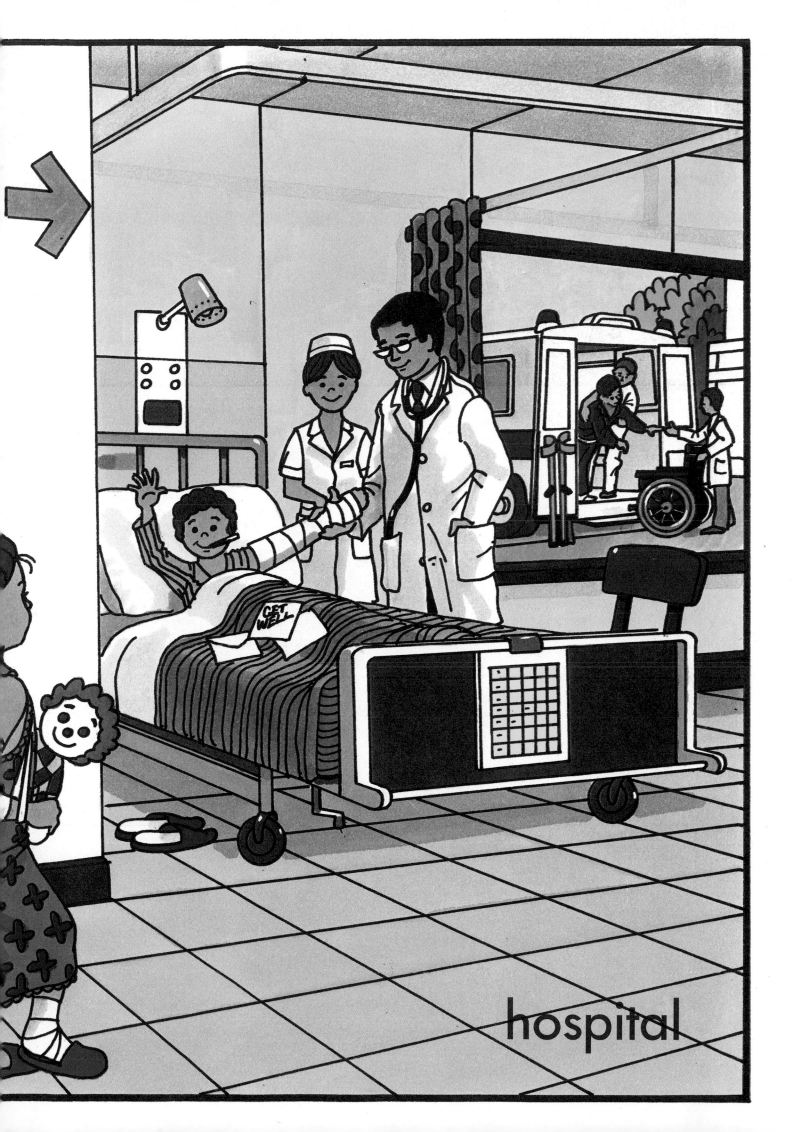

hospital

ZOO

ostrich

elephant

snake

panda

parrot

porcupine

monkey

hippopotamus

dolphin

lion

tiger

kangaroo

zebra

penguin

camel

bear

koala

giraffe

fountain

statue

bench

flower bed

swing

duck

park

roundabout

climbing frame

slide

tree

pond

fence

see-saw

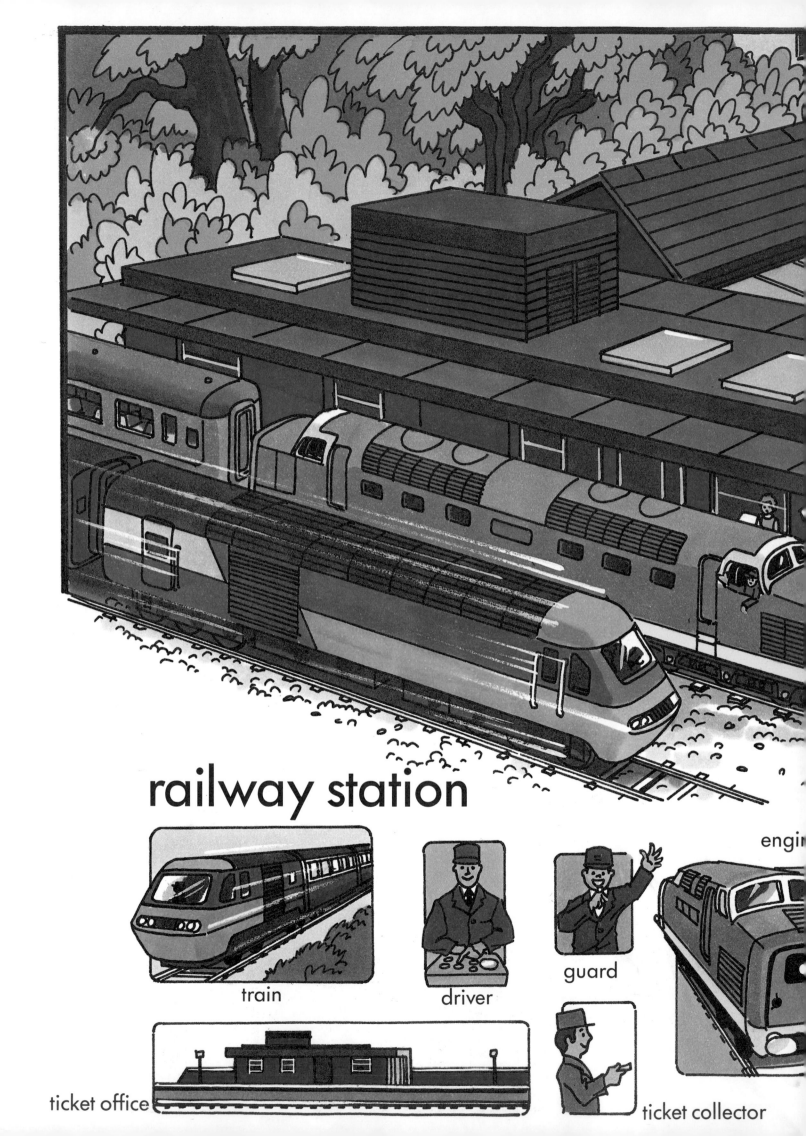

railway station

train

driver

guard

engin

ticket office

ticket collector

bus station

bus

driver

conductor

passengers

queue

destination board

- - - - No. 12
- - - No. 14

dress

t-shirt

shorts

skirt

blouse

jeans

sandals

shoes

boots

hat

gloves

cap

socks

vest

coat

anorak

track suit

shirt

circus

ring master

acrobat

trapeze

sealion

bear

bareback rider

clown

monkey

elephant

dog

juggler

horse

fire station

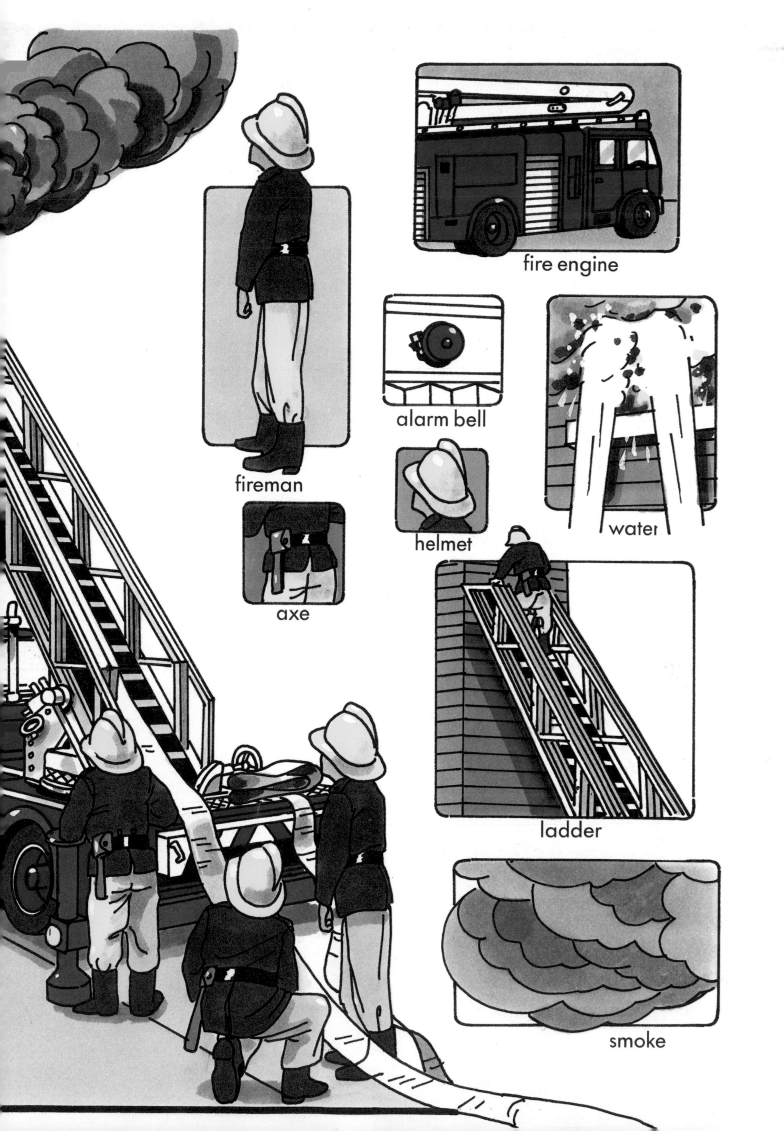

fire engine

fireman

alarm bell

water

helmet

axe

ladder

smoke

seaside

star fish

crab

sun

sand

sea

mask

seaweed

bucket

spade

dinghy

gull

seashells

flippers

flag

swimsuit

brella

deck chair

pebbles

building site

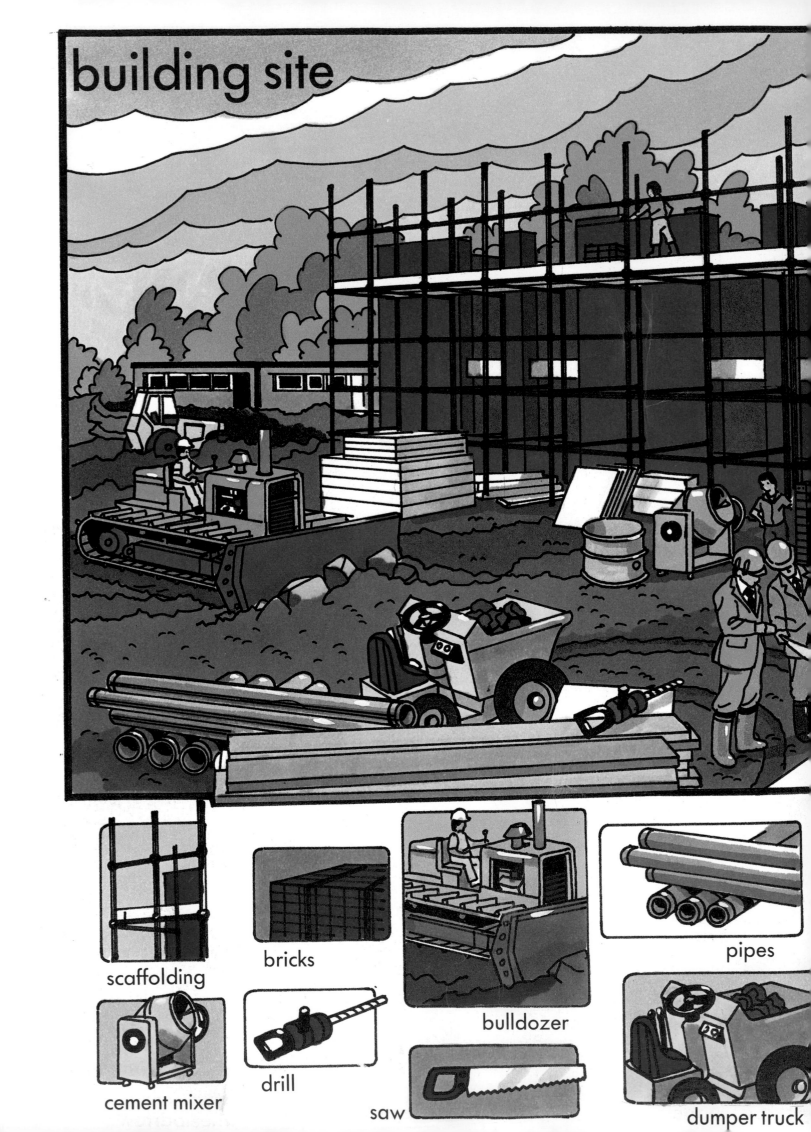

scaffolding

bricks

bulldozer

pipes

cement mixer

drill

saw

dumper truck

tractor

spade

water

crane

wood

hammer

wheelbarrow

food

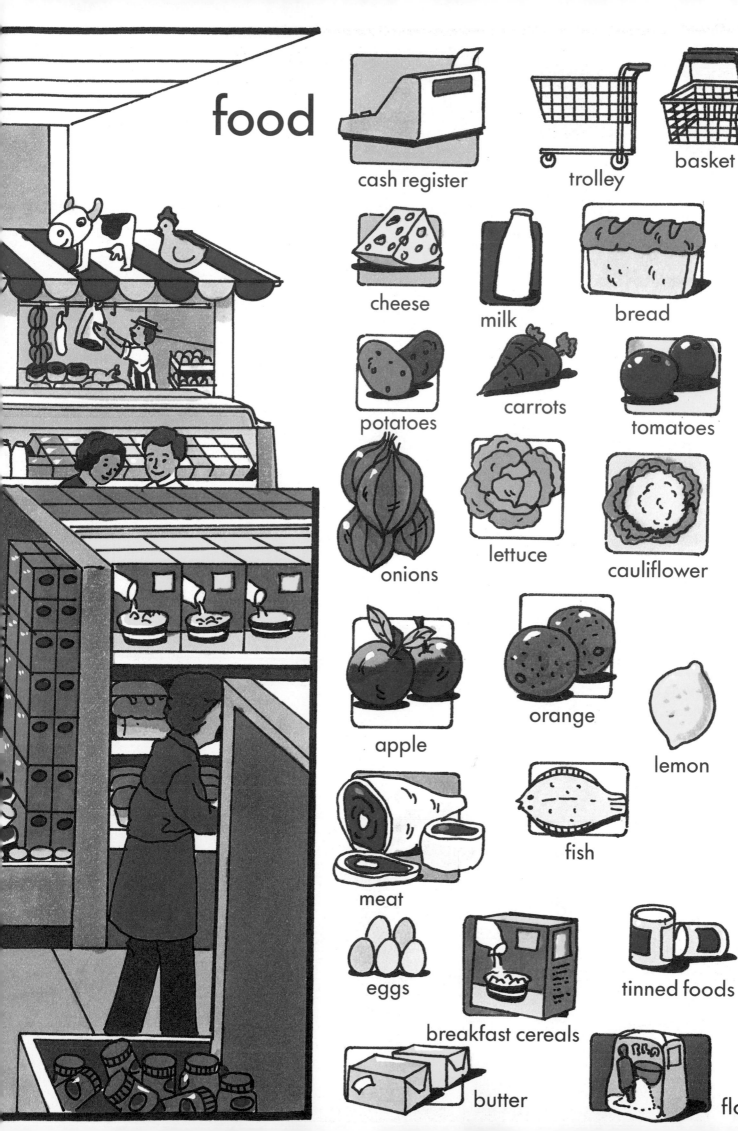

cash register

trolley

basket

cheese

milk

bread

potatoes

carrots

tomatoes

onions

lettuce

cauliflower

apple

orange

lemon

meat

fish

eggs

breakfast cereals

tinned foods

butter

flour

pet shop

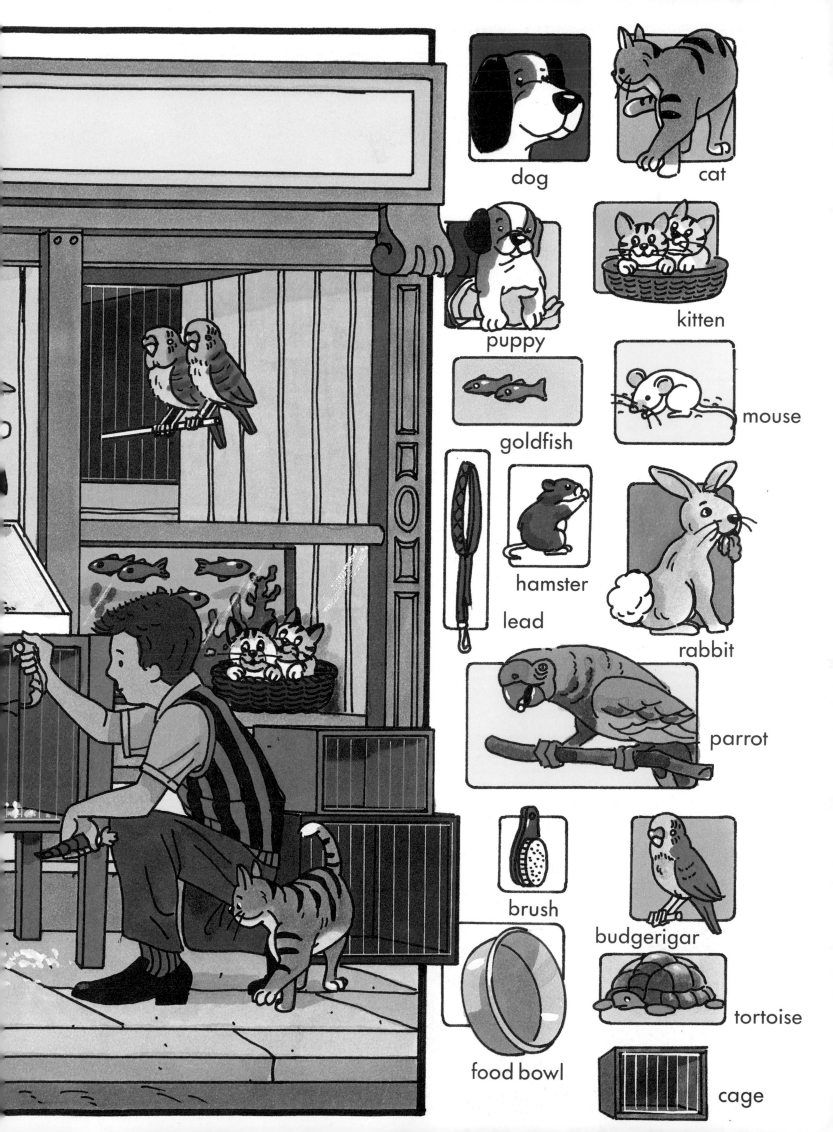

dog

cat

puppy

kitten

goldfish

mouse

hamster

lead

rabbit

parrot

brush

budgerigar

tortoise

food bowl

cage

motorbike

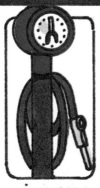

air pump

battery

petrol pump

breakdown lo

oil

petrol tanker

truck

garage

tyres

car

shop

mechanic

engine

word list

acrobat
aeroplane
air hostess
airport
air pump
alarm bell
ambulance
anchor
anorak
apple
axe

ball
bandage
bareback rider
barge
barn
basket
bath
bathroom
battery
bear
bed
bedroom
bench
blackboard
blouse

boat
book
boot
bread
breakdown lorry
breakfast cereal
brick
brush
bucket
budgerigar
building bricks
building site
bulldozer
buoy
bus
bus station
bus stop
butter

cage
calendar
calf
camel
cap
car
carpet
carrot

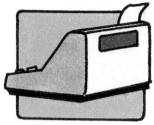

cash register
castle
cat
cauliflower
cement mixer
chair
chalk
chart
check-in desk
cheese
church
cinema
circus
city
climbing frame
clothes
clown

coat
conductor
control tower
cooker
cow
crab
crane
crossing
crutches

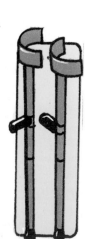

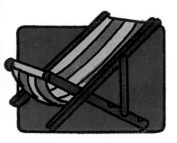

globe
glove
goat
goldfish
guard
gull

deck chair
desk
destination board
dinghy
docker
doctor
dog
doll
dolls' house
dolphin
donkey
door
drawers
drawing pin

factory
farm
farmer
farm house
fence
ferry
field
fire engine
fireman
fire station
fish
fisherman
fishing boat
flag
flats
flippers
flour
flower bed
food
food bowl
fountain
fuel truck

hammer
hamster
hangar
harbour
hat
haystack
helicopter
helmet
hen
hippo
horse
hospital
house
hovercraft

dress
dressing gown
drill
driver
duck
dumper truck

ink

jeans
juggler

kangaroo
kettle
kitchen
kitten
koala

egg
elephant
engine

garage
garden
geese
giraffe

ladder
lamb
landing light
lead
lemon
lettuce
lifebelt
lighthouse
lion
living room
luggage

map
marbles
mask
meat
mechanic
milk
monkey
motorbike
mouse

net
nightdress
nurse

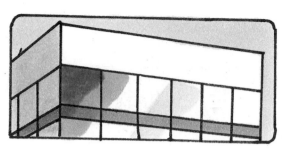

office block
oil
oil tanker
onion
orange
orchard
ostrich

paint
panda
paper
park
parrot
passenger
pebble
pen
pencil
penguin
petrol pump
petrol tanker
pet shop
pig
pilot
pipe
plaster
plough
police car
policeman

pond
porcupine
porter
potatoes
puppet
puppy
pyjamas

queue

rabbit
racing car
railway station
refrigerator
ring master
road sign
robot
rocking horse
roundabout
ruler
runway

sailor
sand
sandals
saw
scaffolding
school
scissors
sea